GARETH EGAN

EXQUISITE
CREATURES

A POETRY COLLECTION

Exquisite Creatures
by Gareth Egan

ISBN: 978-0-646-81550-3

Copyright © 2020 by Gareth Egan

All rights reserved. This book or any portion thereof may not be reproduced or used in any manner whatsoever without the express permission of the publisher except for the use of brief quotations in a book review.

Presented in English

Self-Published.

Front cover illustration
licensed through Shuttershock inc.
all rights reserved by the appropriate copyright holder.

Front cover, typesetting and book design by
Gareth Egan

www.garethegan.com
instagram.com/gareth.egan
instagram.com/garetheganwords

Also by Gareth Egan

THE CHAOS IN-BETWEEN (2018)
THE ANTHEM OF BROKEN HUMANS (2019)

To those amongst us
who wear their hearts
on their sleeve,

to those
who fall in love
too quickly,

and to those
who show us
the pleasures
and pitfalls
of thinking
too hard and
thinking too much;

I know where you ache -

my heart and my mind
steer my life too.

Those who show us
the magic of being human
are the most
exquisite creatures
of us all.

TABLE OF CONTENTS

THE HUMAN CONDITION	4
SPINNING AROUND	6
DIFFERENT OUTLOOK	7
NOT NORMAL	8
MY STORY	10
OVERTHINKER	11
OUR WAR	12
COLOURLESS	13
BODY CLOCK	14
STORY TIME	16
BATTLE ARMOUR	17
HORROR MOVIE	18
BREATHING SPACE	20
FIRST WORLD PROBLEMS	22
INSOMNIA	24
FROM THE DARKNESS WITHIN	25
NIGHT SWEATS	26
HAUNTED	30
HIDING PLACE	31
AN INDECENT PAUSE	32
THE DAILY STRUGGLE	36
BEASTS	37
RESONATING	38
BULLIED	39
YEARS I WOULD LIKE TO FORGET	40
INFOMERCIALS	42
NOTHING TO HIDE	46
FLAWS AND ALL	47
SINNED	48
SUNBURNT	50
CATCH 22	52
UNPREPARED	54

FORBIDDEN WORDS	55
SIMILAR DEMISE	56
THE OTHER SIDE	57
CLEAN WRISTS	58
VENGEANCE	59
GAS-LIGHTED	60
TORN	62
BOTTOMLESS	63
STRANGERS	64
JUMPING AT SHADOWS	65
CELESTIAL ALIGNMENT	66
SENSORY OVERLOAD	68
DISORGANISED MESS	70
NO GOODBYE	72
STARK REALISATION	73
WHERE DOES LOVE GO	74
CLOSURE	76
LULLABIES OF LONELINESS	78
BEDFELLOWS	79
FADE OUT	80
TOO MUCH TO ASK?	82
INNER CHILD	84
TAKE THE TIME	85
UNSCATHED	86
DRY EYES	87
BEAUTIFUL TEACHERS	88
METAMORPHOSIS	90
BLOOM	91
FRACTURED SOULS	92
IMMORTAL UTOPIAS	93
TRIAL AND ERROR	94

NOT SET	95
CENSORSHIP	96
OVER-ANALYSING	98
COME OUT STRONGER	100
NO DIVINE HELP REQUIRED	102
MAJOR VICTORIES	104
RUNNING FROM THE FLAMES	105
FORGIVENESS	106
HOMELESS IN SANITY	107
SCHOOL OF LIFE	108
TO REALLY LIVE	109
MADDENING EXPERIENCES	110
TOO BUSY	111
AT ALL COSTS	112
WAITING	114
WEIGHING UP	116
GIVE IN	118
HONESTLY MAD	119
EAGER TO FIND HOME	120
COMPANIONSHIP	121
NEVER-ENDING	122
ON THE BREEZE	124
TAKING THINGS APART	126
TO A FRIEND IN NEED	128
HAPPY DEMISE	132
AT HOME WITH THE DEVIL	134
TIME TO GO	135
OUR LEGACY	136
THE MAGIC	138
STONE HATS	139

EXQUISITE CREATURES

The Human Condition

The faces and the lives
of other human beings
intrigue me.

I am a people watcher -
a student of
the human condition.

That said -
with all of the knowledge
that I have gained
from all of my pondering -
  the casual glances
  and more in-depth
observations,
what I have discovered
is that every single other
person -
  the pious,
  the sinful,
  the well kept,
  and unkempt alike,
are doing it (life)
a damn sight better
than I am,
and for the life of me
I cannot find a single

definitive or
quantifiable
reason why;

it all seems
so genetically
unfair;

we are all made of
the same substances
and our bodies all
function
in the exact same way.
We even share
99% of the same DNA.

But here I am,
without an answer as to why
I am different,
flailing hopelessly
in the open
grabbing at pieces
of existence
as they flyby
in a vain attempt to
make them fit the puzzle
that is me.

SPINNING AROUND

Maybe I will stop
  spinning around
and maybe
  I will stop for air
but maybe
  I like the head rush
and maybe
  I like the way
  that the terrain ahead
  looks a little
  less harsh
  when I am moving
  a million miles a minute.

Yes, it may only be
a fantasy
held by my inner child
but I sincerely wish
that I could return
to a time
before the age of 6 -

a time when
the world looked
a little less harsh;

spinning or not.

DIFFERENT OUTLOOK

I guess that I
have always
had a different
outlook
on life than most -

I taste colours
differently
   I hear beauty in ways
  others would think crazy.

I guess that it has lead me
to possess a soul
that is slightly
more broken than most,

but that
does not frighten me;

it is my uniqueness
in a world
where everybody
is trying so hard
to be the same.

NOT NORMAL

I do not have
a problem
with the word normal -

I am sure it is
a definition fitting
of a lot of people,
just not me.

We,
normal
and I,
are not opposites,
the truth is that we
are two concepts
that do not
occupy
the same plane -
  ethereal,
   philosophical
    or
   physical.
And rightfully so
because if
I am ever
goingto be happy,
truly happy,

not just temporarily so,
then normal
and I will
remain notions
that remain
beautifully far apart.

That way,
normal
will be at peace
it in its universe
and I
in mine.

MY STORY

I am the only person
that needs
define me;

words,
templates
and the "well intended" advice
of others,
I will tolerate

but when it comes to me,
and who I am,

that is a story
I am writing
and I need
no collaboration
from those
who think
that they know better.

OVERTHINKER

Overthinking
is what I do well,
it is all I know -

overthinking
is the cause of
all of my pain

but to hell
with it
if I am not going to use it
to put to rest
every last bit
of the same.

OUR WAR

The most intense
challenge
that we
will ever face
is the one that
we must
fight
with our own mind.

How scary
a thought it is
that our strongest ally
can so easily
turn against us;

they say -
    that you should
    know your enemy;

they
never told me -
    that it would be
    an inch deep
    within
    my own head.

COLOURLESS

Sadness -

depression,
anxiety,
are not
a blue haze
or
a black dog.

Such states of
existence
are a
colourless mass;

the weight of
which can crush
a human soul.

BODY CLOCK

I am unsure how
I have survived
up until this point -

Madness?
Sanity?

A liberal serving
of both?

No –
I guess,
dying a little
with each heartbeat
is how I have
made it through
this mess -

knowing that
there will be an end
and I will get there
someday.

No matter how sane
or how mad
I am –
we are,

we all
pass away
and that
is our
reprieve

and it is up to us
if we pass
with a smile
on our face
or otherwise.

STORY TIME

Scars
are the stories
that our lives
have written
on our skin.

BATTLE ARMOUR

This poor,
tired
flesh
of mine
has seen its
share of misery.

But still,
morning after morning,
day after day
I cloak
myself in it
to take on
the next incoming
affliction;

it is my shield,
my armour.

I just hope, in time,
that I can learn
to love it, as much as rely on it,
before the beasts
of this burdensome life
wear it away
leaving me bear boned
to the pain.

HORROR MOVIE

A haunting
picture show
is projected,
constantly,
on to the inside of
my eyelids.

Flashes
and movement
visible only
to my minds eye;

Non-celluloid movies
of
  all of the
  mistakes that
  I have made,

of
  all the
  stupid,
  awkward
  times
  that I have
  clumsily
  tripped over
  my own tongue,

and of
   all the idiotic moments
   that I so dreadfully regret.

The images though,
that burn in
the deepest
are not the ones
of what
   I have done
or what
   I have said
but of
   everything
   that I haven't;

the little bits
of magic
within myself
that I have failed
to release
because of that same
haunting
picture show.

BREATHING SPACE

I have tried
waiting,

patiently,

but this
anxiety
riddled
mind of mine
will not allow me
to rest with
any degree
of peace;

I am screaming
for tomorrow
so much that
I am letting today
pass me by.

And, in that,
a dilemma
has been manifested -

I am not only
anxious
for what is to come

but for what is
a non-existent
now;

all I hunger for
is space
from this
anxious mind
allowing me
a little time
to breathe.

FIRST WORLD PROBLEMS

I am
tragically
a victim of
the first world -

I have
too much
  choice,

I have
too much
  free will,

I am
too scared
  to make a decision,

I am
too scared
  to succeed.

I am
not blaming
anyone else
for my own
shortcomings -

I take
full ownership
of the situation
that I
find myself
in;

I have contracted
the condition
of the day
and feel
hopelessly alone
whilst still being
surrounded
by a billion
other people
who feel
exactly the same.

INSOMNIA

2am.

Alone,

in the darkness

and the walls
recount
all of my failures
to me;

and how heavy
have they become
in the early hours
of the morning.

FROM THE DARKNESS WITHIN

And it is not
the dark itself
that frightens me -

it harbours none
of my enemies,

there is no boogie man,
no entity,
waiting to jump out
and grab me.

No,

my demons have
taken roost
in the darkness
within me
and it is there
where
they lay in wait,
ready to pounce;

it is just a coincidence
that they often wait,
to do so,
until the sky falls dark.

NIGHT SWEATS

The middle of the night
quite often scares me;

the anxiety of it all.

I occasionally
forget how
to write

and, more than regularly,
I forget how to sleep.

And, sometimes,
I even forget how to breathe.

The whole damn
situation scares me.

My mind a flutter -
of thoughts.
of fears.
of unfounded self-torture.

I wonder.
    I wonder.
I wonder.
    I wonder

which causes which-

Is it the lack of oxygen to the brain?
the lack of sleep?
a lack of writing talent
that causes my anxiety?

Or
is it the anxiety itself
manifesting in the most
horrid of ways.

Depriving me of
what I want
and what I need.

It hasn't always
been that way.

Night time,
early mornings -
the hours after dark
and before sunlight.

Dark streets.
Neon shop lights.

Traffic signals.
Cool breezes;
Car indicators
blinking
on damp roads.

Such spectacles
once excited me.

They invited a sense
of curiosity,
a sense
of a world
that has slowed down
but still moving;
the only fear
being that
of missing out.

Now,
I just hide -

Not writing.

Not sleeping.

Not breathing.

With the overwhelming
fear
that I will
permanently
lose the cognitive
ability to remember
how to do all three;

especially the latter -

the ability
to breathe.

HAUNTED

Have you ever
cried out.
at night.
for someone
who is no longer there -

to someone
who could not call back?

I have
at times
screamed to myself
from within my slumber;

I left long ago
and
miss being me -

a fact that haunts
my sleep.

HIDING PLACE

There is a place
I go when I am
feeling vulnerable
and that is within
myself -

if I ever seem distant,
or it appears
as if I don't care,
it is only because
I care too much.

I am trying to find
the sense amongst
the madness
and interpret
it in my own way;

all I need is time
and understanding;

I hope that you
will still be here
when I return.

AN INDECENT PAUSE

My life,
at least for
the last five years,
feels as as if
it has fallen victim
to the most indecent
of pauses -

the most draining
form of inaction
that I
have ever encountered;

I know that I
have to dig deep
and get
my life
going again.

I know that I
cannot wait
for another person,
or a specific moment,
to give me
a push and
get the ball
rolling.

I know I have it in me
to fight -

to vanquish
what it is
that holds me back
and,
at last,
put all of
my irrationalities
to rest.

Yes,
it is more
than true
that I know
what needs to be done,

I could even write down
on paper
a list of the exact
actions to take
and their outcomes,

and I am just as well aware
that it needs
to happen now,

however,

poetically tragic,

in the haste
of wanting
to live
for today
I have become
so anxious
for any type
of momentum
that even
the resonance
of my own heart
shakes
me to the core -

life giver, life taker -

a dreadful
contradiction
that turns even the most
minor of efforts
into an
insurmountable
disaster;

my future
and who I am
slowly becoming
collateral damage;

I, myself
the perpetrator
and
the victim.

THE DAILY STRUGGLE

Hello
tiny fallen
angels
hiding inside my
bones;

shall we fight
each other
one more day

or shall we sleep
the pain
away?

BEASTS

I wish to know
what you think of
as you lay alone
at night.

I wish to know
what haunts you
and shakes
you from your sleep.

I wish touch you deeply,
lulling
into fatal submission
the beasts
that have nested
inside you;

I wish to love
you free.

RESONATING

The sun
farewells
the streets
outside
and
your words
resonate
in my mind;

if only they
had of been
a little more kind,
a little less jagged

then, I would
be able to
lay
my head
down,
to rest,
a little
lighter

than the
heaviness
that consumes
me now.

BULLIED

And how toxic
have the words
that you spoke
to an 8 year old me,

become in the dark;

words that still
trigger the type
of emotions
that you hoped
they would.

that still echo through
my mind;
    many.
        many.
            many.
years later.

YEARS I WOULD LIKE TO FORGET

There are many years
I would like
to forget

I am 34 -
There really
hasn't been
a hell of a lot
that I've had

but
the majority,

I would like
to throw to
dark abandonment;

to the fuzzy
patches
in the back of
my brain
that store
useless,
unneeded,
undeserved
pieces
of information.

But,
in such an undertaking,
I struggle
terribly;

it is 2020
and I am still
being haunted
by 1993.

INFOMERCIALS

3:12am

and the late
night
infomercials
are telling me
that I am unworthy
    of loving
and unworthy
    of living.

They tell me I need
    tighter abs.
They tell me I need
    to loose 20kgs,
They tell me I need
    a better car,
    a better knife set,
    a better ladder;

    a better life.

And in the daze
that is another
sleepless
night
I keep listening,

allowing the
fast talking
spruikers
to convince me
to evaluate my life.

Sure,
    I could do with
    losing some weight.

Sure,
    I do need
    a new car.

Sure
    I guess maybe I do need
    a ladder that is 50
    scaffolding
    solutions in 1;

but my
commonsense -

my lucid,
yet restless,
10 am self
tells me

that
I am good
 enough.
I am worth
 loving.
I am worth
 living.

He tells
me that
all of
the hypnotic
hyperbole
defecating
from my
Television
is marketing -

cash thirsty
companies
preying
on the fragile
minds
and weak
hearts
that occupy
the early mornings.

And I know
that he is right -

he always is;

I just wish
I was awake
more often
at 10
than I am at 2.

NOTHING TO HIDE

Quite often
my emotions
are a little
too naked
for you
to deal with
and that's OK,

naked is OK;

I have nothing
to hide
and no means
in which to hide them
even if I did.

FLAWS AND ALL

I stand here
raw,
naked.
(all too) fragile
and vulnerable

I ask you to see
me for me

and appreciate me
for my flaws
as much as my
redeeming qualities;

I am a three dimensional
and whole human;

any other form
would be flat
bland
unexciting
and very un-me.

SINNED

Humans,

like you
and I

have had to learn
to spell
our words
with a grin -

a smile
that hides
the fact that we
have been scarred
by other people's
sins.

TIRED

This warrior heart
of mine
needs to rest

it has come under
attack too many times -

mostly against
itself;

this warrior heart
of mine needs to rest.

SUNBURNT

Physically,
I have lived
as close
to the surface
of the sun
as any other human
that has ever
existed
before me,

but
in my own
mind
I feel as though
I have been
scorched
a little more
than anyone else;

maybe
it is because
I have the most
fierce
of fires
wanting to
break free
from within me

or quite possibly,
it is because
not many
other people
know what it is like
to live with
the stars
inside of them
and fear letting
the light out
as much as I do.

CATCH 22

There is
no more
a bitter-sweet
situation
than to be
lost
within your
own mind.

On one hand
   you
   are seemingly
   free
   from that which
   haunts you
   on the outside.

on the other -

   you remain
   desperately
   a prisoner,

   hopelessly
   victimised
   by your own
   thoughts -

thoughts -

   thoughts that
   are never
   entirely silent;
   never overtly loud -

   an uncomfortable
   middle ground
   that slowly
   torments
   and enslaves;

if only
you could decide
if you wanted
to escape or to stay;

in some ways
you would be
fighting and
capitulating
on both counts
irrespective
of your decision;

catch 22.

UNPREPARED

I do not blame you
for my state of mind

nor do I blame
your absence
on my state of mind.

The two are
independent
concerns;

not victims
of each-other

but victims of
a fight
that neither were
ready for.

FORBIDDEN WORDS

What a dream
it was
to be loved by you

and what
a nightmare
it was
to have you
forget
the sound
of my name.

SIMILAR DEMISE

How many times
must I die

before you see

that you
and I -

we,

break the same?

THE OTHER SIDE

Walking out the door
was the easy part

leaving you
on the
other side
will continue to
haunt me
each and every
time I leave
a room.

CLEAN WRISTS

I wear
my heart
on my sleeve

and your words
belong
nowhere
near my wrists.

VENGEANCE

I have no eye
on revenge;

I will write my path
in love
and be driven down
it by the same.

GAS-LIGHTED

You
have had
me
questioning
my worth,
my mind,
my very place
in existence;

what I
am no longer
questioning
is whether you
and
your type
of energy
belong
in my life -

both do not;

a realisation
that has
taken
me
all too long
to reach.

So here, today,
I pledge
with a thunderous,
yet silent,
internal scream
that you
and your toxicity -

your gas-lighting ways,

are dead to me,

they will no longer
stain my days
and from them
I shall finally
set myself free,

TORN

I am torn -
I do not know
if I should
be mourning
the loss of the humans
that we were
when we first met
or celebrating
the knowledge
that we will never be
the people that
we had become;

I love you,
I miss you,
but I think this
is our time to reflect,
to heal
and to grow -

for ourselves
and
for nobody else.

BOTTOMLESS

We are both
victims of desire -

we wanted so much
'to be'

that we never really
looked as deep into
each other
as we should have;

our love sat
on the surface

and only passion
willing to sink
to the bottom
of oceans
should ever be
plundered.

STRANGERS

One day,
I will forget
what it is like
to feel
the way that I do
for you;

I just hope
there will never come
a time
where the recollections
of who we were
fade in the same way;

I fear
that if
that reality
ever arrives,
we will become
nothing more
than two strangers,
who were only
passing time.

JUMPING AT SHADOWS

Sometimes,
I see ghosts
and other times
I am just jumping
at shadows.

What I now know is
they aren't
spectres
from another realm,

but fragments
of you leaving
me for good.

CELESTIAL ALIGNMENT

There was once
a time
that it was simple
to say
I love you.

Now it takes

all of
   the planets,

all of
   the moons

and all of
   the stars

to align
to even say hello.

The simple fact is
that you were once
my universe
and no amount
of time or distance
can ever
change that;

one day
there will be
a celestial alignment
and we will
speak again,

but for now -

I will have to be
satisfied
looking up
at the sky
patiently
waiting.

SENSORY OVERLOAD

I have always
found it
amazing
how a
triggering
of one of
our senses
can draw out
memories
from another -

a sight
triggering
a smell -
a smell
a sound.

That is why
it is so hard
to talk to you
at the moment -

the sound of
your voice
reminds me
too much
of the taste of

your skin
and how
I wrote
my hopes
and dreams
for our future
across it
with my lips.

Hopes
and dreams
that are now
only memories -

memories
that smell like
loss
and taste like
tears.

DISORGANISED MESS

Honestly,

what constitutes
a name?

an organised grouping
of letters -

vowels,
consonants
turned into words
and rolled around
the tongue;

nothing really.

No different than
any other word
in any of the 6,500
other languages
on earth.

Why then,
when yours
is still uttered,
does it chill
each bone

that runs down
my spine?
I guess,
if I try and
pinpoint
an exact
explanation
it is because
a name
is so much
more than an
organised
grouping
of letters;

it is a moniker
for a disorganised
mess
of flesh and soul.

NO GOODBYE

There was no
goodbye -

one day
you were mine
and the next
you were not;

as if our two existences
had never
come into contact;

as if yours was a world
I had never visited
and mine was
one you couldn't
put a name to;

once we were
us
and then we were
strangers.

STARK REALISATION

When we lose what
we thought was ours
we begin to love
it more;

as time has passed
I have begun to
comprehend that
you were never mine

and I –

well,

I was never yours.

WHERE DOES LOVE GO

I think,
I know what
true love is
and I think,
that we
may have
shared it,

but what is it
that we have now
that we are
no longer
in love
with who
each other are?

Does love
fade?

Does it
disappear?

or does it
lay
dormant,
waiting to be
rekindled?

What ever
happens
to such
emotions,
I hope that
I am not a
a hopeless
romantic
to believe
that we may
find them again;

if not in
each other,
then,
maybe -

as sad it is to say,

in other
people.

CLOSURE

I would be
lying
if I was to say
that I won't
always carry a part of
you with me;

deep,
unspoken,
underneath
my ribs.

And even with
the hindsight
of time,

to say that
I don't miss you,
would be
unfair,

and, well,
untrue -

but, to utter
such words -
aloud,

or to myself,

would only
undo
the decisions
that we have made,

burdening
the lives
that we
now have
for ourselves.

So, with the time
that has passed,
and the healing
that it has brought

I hope that we
have both
found closure;

and that these
words
can serve
as my final
adieu.

LULLABIES OF LONELINESS

I have become
too well
acquainted
with the
lullabies
of loneliness
that rattle
in my head.

My only
solace
from
solitude
being the
delirium
that they
dance me into –

a twisted
tango
for one.

BEDFELLOWS

I have fallen
into bed
with my solitude
and I am finding it
impossible
to pull
myself up
and out
from underneath
the covers.

FADE OUT

I am forever
surrounded
by an abundance
of beautiful
souls;

all
   matched up
all
   cheek to cheek
all
   moving in rhythm.

Instead of
admiring
the movement
and music of
such a display
the imagery
leaves me empty;

the realisation being
that my own
soul
still traipses
without
a match.

I am alone
 I am tired
  I am empty

all I want
is to lay down
and close my eyes
in the hope that
I can escape
long enough
for the song
to eventually end.

TOO MUICH TO ASK?

I often ponder as to why
I am still single

and sadly,
I keep coming
to the same conclusion;

this world
is not yet ready to love me -

it is still trying
to get over the
pitiful shallowness
that plagues it.

Such a dilemma
that leaves me to ask
if it is too big an effort
from minds that are
burdened with
superficial characteristics,
to love with their hearts
and not with their eyes;

if it is too much
to want those same minds
to love me for me;

is it too much
to propose such a love
when beautifully raw
heart bleeders
are left to die alone?

maybe the day
that they finally do
occupy themselves
with more than
the material
will be the day that I

will find love again;

until then,
I will have to
be content with
loving me for who I am,

and that,
for better or
for worse,

may be the only love
that I will ever
need find.

INNER CHILD

Where you see an adult
that is slightly broken,
I see a child that had been
completely broken -

a soul who had
been shattered to pieces,
but was still able
to muster the strength
within themselves
that it takes
to find their way
in spite of all the odds;

a human being
grateful for
nothing more
than being able
to wake up one morning
after the next;

an ability we take
for granted -
one they had to fight for.

TAKE THE TIME

Before you judge me,
take two minutes
(it really isn't a lot of time),
and sit with me,

Put one hand on your chest
and the other on mine
and ask yourself
have you walked each step
with a heart beat
in sync with mine?

Well, until you do
there is no possible way
for you to know that which
I have gone through.

UNSCATHED

If you have never
been lost,
If you have never
been broken,

I feel sorry for
you,
as you have never felt
the sting
from the beautiful
catastrophes of life;

and if there is
one lesson
that I have learnt
it is that there
is very little allure
in an unscathed soul.

DRY EYES

Thank you
for showing me
that tears
are only ever shed
to be dried.

BEAUTIFUL TEACHERS

And If we are
truly lucky,

then once,
or twice
in a lifetime,

we have the chance
to meet someone
who will change
our lives in the most
important of ways -

be it a small,
or a large gesture,

they open us up to
all types of uniqueness
that have us growing
and evolving from who we
thought we were.

Talk to strangers -
lay your ears and
your minds open
to those who have
lived,

lost and loved before you -

listen
   to their stories,
listen
   to their songs,
listen
   to their lessons;

don't switch yourself off
to that which you don't know;

embrace all that
they are trying
to teach you.

In their failures
you may learn
something to fight
off your demons,

in their successes
the building blocks
to guarantee
your dreams.

METAMORPHOSIS

At the moment,
it may feel like
you are dying inside
but the truth of
the matter is that
you are shedding
the darkest parts
of your past
so that the light
that you crave
has room to enter
your soul.

BLOOM

There is one hell
of a sunrise
inside of you
waiting to
bloom
upon humanity.

I just hope
that you are
not too locked
into an endless
dusk
of your own despair.

I hope
that you can
grant yourself
the permission
to let go of all
that holds you back
and
allow yourself
to bloom.

FRACTURED SOULS

Our souls
are born
along with
all of the bones
in our body

and then,

by 1000 different
means,

both are slowly
broken;

stay strong
sweet child -

stay strong;

bones mend
and so too,
will you.

IMMORTAL UTOPIAS

I think that we
all lose
our innocence
the first time
we realise
that eventually
we will all die;

Before that -
we are all
invincible.

We are all
immortal;

nothing will hurt us,

and nothing
will ever end
our perfect
little
utopias.

TRIAL AND ERROR

There was a time -
not all too long ago.

I would have rather
stared at shadows
on the wall,
than look into
the mirror
and admit
that the reflection
was me.

Succumbing to all of
the joys
and pitfalls
of trial and error,

I have discovered
that to love
myself
    in spite of
my flaws
    was to love
the light
    through the
darkness
that had set in.

NOT SET

Our paths
are not set
in stone

they are much more
fluid
and we can
freeze them, put them
on hold until we
are ready to move forward

or we can swim straight
through
straight towards what it is
that we desire the most.

CENSORSHIP

There is very little
that we
can do about
our past;

what's done
is done.

In fact,
at times,
it feels as if
the only
action
that we
can take
is to bury
deep down
all of
the drama
and
the heartache.

But if we were to do
just that -

censor our own
memories,

would it not
serve
an injustice
to who we
have become?

What I like
to think is
that we can
build ourselves
a future that
celebrates success
and champions loss
as the learning curve
that it has been.

I would rather
remember it all
and grow from it,

than let
the hurt
sink deep
into the bile
and corrode at me
from inside.

OVER-ANALYSING

I've been told that I
analyse things
too much.

I live in
my head.

I read
somethings
into nothings
and then,
let those
nothings,
that are now
somethings,
haunt me;

If I were to listen
to those
evaluations,
and change
my ways -

would I not become

careless,
heartless,

soulless -
without a love
for the world
and a deeper understanding
of how life works?

would I cease to be
able to put my pen
to paper and bleed
the way that I do?

I will continue to
live in my head
for as long as I am me;

If not, if I do listen,
give in,
and change,

then you will
never hear
another word
from me.

COME OUT STRONGER

Although
it was not
an easy journey
you found
yourself on

- at times
a marathon,

you
have come out
the other side
much
stronger;

a living,
breathing
personification
of how
hate
will never
find itself
a purpose
in this world;

your own
struggle -

a more than
elegant
example of
how a soul
can break
and be reborn
to break
the world
that broke it.

NO DIVINE HELP REQUIRED

As much as
I would love
to believe
in the magic
of miracles
and divine
intervention,

I would much rather
put my faith
and patience
in hard work
and perseverance;

I am in control
of my
own direction.

Any omnipotent
assistance
would mean
that I
am living on
borrowed time
in the service
of an
unforeseen master;

I would
much rather
be responsible
for my own
failings

and in turn
claim
ownership
of my own
successes.

MAJOR VICTORIES

Even the most minor
of dilemmas
can tear us apart
on the harshest
of days,

but only when we survive
the storm
that is the toughest parts
of life,

and come
out stronger,

can we then
be justified
crying over
the small
defeats.

RUNNING FROM THE FLAMES

There have been
many little brush fires
in my life
that I have
already faced
and it scares me
to own up to the amount
that I have
run away from;

what I am
willing to admit
is that I have been burnt -

at times by my own hand;

but like flames
through a forest,
there will be regrowth
and I will be born again
to fight the next blaze;

stronger for
all the times that I have
failed to tend off
the flames.

FORGIVENESS

Life isn't
about forgiving
yourself for
making mistakes.

The fact is that
the oppositeis true.

Life is about
forgivingyourself
for not making
enough of them;

We can only ever discover
our strengths,
by first discovering
our weaknesses:

and what an
exhilarating achievement
it is to succeed
by picking
yourself up
after
    falling
and
    falling again.

HOMELESS IN SANITY

How staggering
a struggle
it is to maintain
sanity;

and what a relief
the revelation is,

that when we finally
do break,

we discover
madness
is the only form
of existence
we could ever wish
to occupy.

SCHOOL OF LIFE

The only education
that I have ever needed
has been in
life,
love
and how to survive
both.

Win.
   Fail.
      Fall.

The trials and tribulations
of the brittle (yet brave)
hearted
are where I have gained
my knowledge;

any structured lesson
would be a gratuitous display
from those who haven't
a single idea
of how life is really lived.

TO REALLY LIVE

I would rather
lay here
  wounded,
    broken,
      bleeding,

than live
a sheltered life.

Those who have
never suffered
such turmoil
should
be pitied -

the poor saps
have never
  lived,
never
  loved
and
doubtfully ever will.

MADDENING EXPERIENCES

The most
maddening
experiences
are the most
beautiful;

it takes a true lover
to french kiss insanity
and come out stronger.

TOO BUSY

I would love
to give myself
into loving
another
human being

but
my mind
is too busy,

my heart
too heavy;

both occupied
trying
to fall in love
with me.

AT ALL COSTS

There are far
fewer
finer
maladies
in life than love.

The finest of all
being the love
for one's self.

And,
if I am to consider
the magnitude
of it fully,
that is why
it is the hardest of all
to find.

Many of us,
even the most
grounded,
become unhinged
in the pursuit
of such a love

and that is
the most beguiling

wonderful
part about
such a quest -

we willingly
sacrifice our wits,
for the facet
of life
that counts
the most.

WAITING

I haven't
near enough
reasons
to tie me to
this one
particular spot
on the map;

regardless
I feel
so inexplicably
drawn
to staying
right where
I am;

it could be
that I
have grown
comfortable
staying
stagnate

or

it could be
that I am

earnestly
waiting
for my star
to fall
from the sky
above
in the hope
that love will
at last
find me.

WEIGHING UP

Please don't
misunderstand me
when I
talk about
love
and being
alone;
it is not
that I haven't
experienced
the good
and
the bad
aspects of each;

I have.

I truthfully feel
that the cons
of love

(and anyone who
has been
in love
will tell you
that there
are plenty),

outweigh all
of the pros
that can be offered
from any form
of loneliness.

So, with that knowledge
in mind,
I am happy to profess
that love
is the state that
I hope to live out
my days.

GIVE IN

Hand yourself
over to love,

you may face
its heat
but holding onto
loneliness
means that
you will risk
facing an
existence of endless
hibernation.

We are warm
blooded animals,

do as nature intended;

chase the warmth
and let it
set your blood to high.

HONESTLY MAD

There is a
certain truth
in madness
that is all
too absent
in love;

those that are mad
tend to admit it,

whereas those
that are in love
will never
surrender the fact
that they are
insane enough
to give their dreams
a face;

I am mad
and I am honest -
I'd much rather
be in denial.

EAGER TO FIND HOME

My ache for flesh
has never
been as strong
as my
yearning to
find a little
of myself
in another soul;

you can call me
sapiosexual

but I would
prefer it if you
called me
eager
to find home.

COMPANIONSHIP

I am not desperate
and as alone
as I may feel,

I really do not
'need' anybody,

nor do I overwhelmingly
'want' anybody either;

The fact is
that I am tired
of walking
this winding path
by myself
and want to share
the hills
and the dips
with a heart
that is as patchwork
as mine.

NEVER-ENDING

I can't
find love.

I search for it
and yet
it eludes me.

I am shaking
each tree -
hoping it falls
into my hands.

I am turning
every stone
that I stumble over
in case it has been
hiding

I am even
screaming
at deafening
decibels
capable of shaking
each
and every
potential lover
from their sleep

but still
I cannot
find love.

Maybe my dreams of
such connections
have been corrupted by
movies and TV ;

Maybe such fairytales
are not meant
for someone like me;

all I know is
that, god damn,
at times
I get so lonely.

ON THE BREEZE

I know that
there is someone
out there
for me;

I can feel them.

I can taste,
hear,
smell
and
almost see them
on the breeze.

The wind
reminds me
that a human
does indeed
exist,
not because
of me
but to be part
of me.

Joined
in love,
in life.

And until
the day
that the wind
whisks them
into my direction
I will continue
to let the air
lap at my face
and tell me
stories of
love's
existence.

TAKING THINGS APART

I have forever
been fascinated
with the act
of taking
objects apart -

the peeling back
of solid exteriors
to reveal every
spring,
mechanism,
gear
and cog
that lay
underneath.

If I am ever lucky enough
I will one day
encounter
a person
who is willing
to strip
the flesh from
my own
hard shouldered
facade
in the hopes

of discovering
the mechanics
that lay inside;

I will then
at last
hopefully have an explanation
for every
anxious
heartbeat
and exasperated
breath
that has gone into
creating me.

TO A FRIEND IN NEED

I cannot
tell you
how
to live your life
and
I would never
attempt to;

the only advice
that I
can offer
is that
there is no
road map,
no preordained
order to existence;

life happens,

and as is well known
to all of us -

shit happens;

it is how we
deal with it
that matters.

If you
can ride out
the bumps,

as well as the dips,

happily saying,
that when
the day is over,

that you wish
to wake again
tomorrow,

then it hasn't
been too hard
a battle at all;

it is the times

when you cannot
say for sure

that you
would miss
rising
one more time,

that you
need to stick
your head
down
and do whatever
it takes
to pull yourself
out of the slump
that you
find yourself in;

cry,
   yell,
      get angry
          and scream -

do all
that needs doing

to lift yourself up,

brush yourself off

and prepare
yourself
to fight
again.

I for one
can say
that I
would feel
your loss
if you
ceased to exist;

never stop
the fight,

win at all costs

and never let
the bastards
hold you down.

HAPPY DEMISE

Yes,
it may seem
incredibly
macabre to you,
but when my
time arrives
I want to die
laughing.

I do not see
any sense of
accomplishment in -

as most people
hope for -

dying whilst
asleep;

I want to know
my time is over

and I want it
to happen in a
moment of
pure
happiness;

our final
breathes
are inevitable,

they will arrive,
and much sooner
than any of us
would like,

so why not go
out in a state
that has taken
so long to achieve.

AT HOME WITH THE DEVIL

And If,
when we do die,
it has all
not panned out
as we would
have liked,

I think that we
can take
some comfort
in the fact
that we will be
the most
adjusted
souls in hell;

we have
spent this lifetime
becoming
well acquainted
with such
rapture.

TIME TO GO

And when
the reaper does
arrive
at my door -

40, 50, 60
years from now.

I will be smiling.
knowing that I
have fought
for my happiness
and that the fight
was worth it.

OUR LEGACY

There is no thought
more primal
than the contemplation
of our own
mortality.

The inclination
that some time soon -

in the scheme of time
that is our short stay
on this planet,

that all of the laughter
and torture
we have endured
will be laid to waste.

The one certainty is that
there will come
a day that all of us -

the brilliant
and even
the ordinary
will pass from
this realm.

And it is our legacy -

the one that
out lives
our mortal
body,

that defines who
who we are -
who we were

and we had
better hope
that it is one
that sees more than
blank looks
on the faces of those
who are left to remember
that we existed at all.

THE MAGIC

And all the tears.

All the smiles.

All the failures.

All the wins.

All the overcoming
of adversity (and
getting into it
in the first place)
is the magic
and we -

we are merely
students of the biggest
lesson of all.

STONE HATS

Work hard.

Be honest.

Follow your dreams

and when
the dust from your bones
returns to the earth
you may be remembered
as more than
a name on a stone.

www.garethegan.com
instagram.com/gareth.egan

#garethegan
#exquisitecreatures

www.ingramcontent.com/pod-product-compliance
Lightning Source LLC
Chambersburg PA
CBHW070306010526
44107CB00056B/2500